FRENCHTOWN

FRENCHTOWN

A DRAMA ABOUT SHANGHAI, P.R.C.

Lawrence Jeffery

EXILE
editions

Library and Archives Canada Cataloguing in Publication

Jeffery, Lawrence, 1953–
    Frenchtown : a drama about Shanghai, P.R.C. / Lawrence Jeffery.

ISBN 978-1-55096-302-1

I. Title.

PS8569.E44F74 2012   C812'.54   C2012-906212-X

Published by Exile Editions Ltd ~ www.ExileEditions.com
144483 Southgate Road 14 – GD, Holstein, Ontario, N0G 2A0
Printed and Bound in Canada by Imprimerie Gauvin, 2012

The publisher would like to acknowledge the financial support of the Canada
Council for the Arts, the Government of Canada through the Canada Book Fund
(CBF), the Ontario Arts Council, and the Ontario Media Development Corpora-
tion, for our publishing activities.

Conseil des Arts du Canada   Canada Council for the Arts

ONTARIO ARTS COUNCIL
CONSEIL DES ARTS DE L'ONTARIO

Canadä

Ontario
Ontario Media Development Corporation

The author can be contacted at: lawrencejeffery@hotmail.com.
Inquiries regarding publication, translation, or film rights: info@exileeditions.com

Canadian Sales: The Canadian Manda Group, 165 Dufferin Street,
Toronto ON M6K 3H6   www.mandagroup.com   416 516 0911

North American and International Distribution, and U.S. Sales:
Independent Publishers Group, 814 North Franklin Street,
Chicago IL 60610   www.ipgbook.com   toll free: 1 800 888 4741

for
Anson Chan Fang On-sang
with gratitude
and abiding affection

FRENCHTOWN

SHANGHAI, P.R.C. – 1995

CHARACTERS

KATE   Born in the USA. Caucasian. In her 70s.

DJ   Born in Canada. Caucasian. In his early 40s.

CAT   Born in the P.R.C. Chinese. In her late 20s.

HONGYONG (Grand & Courageous) CAT's son. He is 10.

SAM*   Born in the P.R.C. Chinese. In his early 30s.

JAMES   Born in Canada. Caucasian. In his late 70s.

RONGJI*   (Solid Foundation) Born in the P.R.C. Chinese. He is 45.

*RONGJI and SAM can be played by the same actor.

Act I Scene I

*The sitting room of a flat on the second floor of a three-storey apartment build-
ing in Shanghai's former French Concession. The building was built in the 1920s.
The ceilings are high. The walls are grey. The room is dark. The room is cluttered
with dusty Chinese antiquities—rolled-up carpets, cabinets, screens, tables and
lamps. Some objects are rare and precious, others are oddly common, tattered and
cheap. Nothing is done to draw attention to the objects. All are displayed as if pos-
sessing equal rarity or beauty. It is difficult to understand the logic behind the col-
lection. Is this a sophisticated collector or a compulsive collector who happens—
from time to time—to stumble upon a real treasure?*

*Nothing in the flat works properly. Lamps must be turned on or off by screwing
or unscrewing the light bulb. Some telephones work better than others—all are
battered and old. And their plugs are in constant danger of disconnection. The
heating comes on or turns off according to its own logic.*

*KATE is in her mid 70s, tall and strong. She was born in the USA. She speaks
with a hybrid accent—modified by the foreign languages she speaks and the
decades she has spent living outside the United States. To her left is a dog basket
covered in a blanket. RUBY, her ancient Shih Tzu sleeps under the blanket. The
only source of heat is an electrical unit high up on the wall to her left. When the
heat comes on it blows warm air across the top of the room. Red ribbons are
attached to the unit. They float out and flutter on the warm air. There is a large
oval* oeil-de-boeuf *window behind KATE's right shoulder. Through the window we see a patch of sky, the edge of a roof and the white wall of the building
across the alley. Oddly, it seems as if the sky, the roof and the building wall seen
through the window are in colour while the interior of the flat is in black and
white.*

KATE sits on a large sofa centre stage facing the audience. She is wrapped in a blanket against the cold. A lamp arches over her shoulder illuminating a book she reads. She wears glasses and holds a magnifying glass. She wears gloves with the tips of the fingers cut off. Books litter the sofa and spill onto the floor.

(A buzzer sounds once—harsh and aggressive)

SILENCE

(The buzzer sounds again)

SILENCE

(The buzzer sounds. The note is held for five seconds. KATE looks up from her book, she reaches over and picks up the telephone)

KATE: Wei? Ni-hao. Hello? *(She hangs up the telephone. The buzzer sounds twice—two short bursts of noise. KATE rises from the sofa—throwing off the blanket as she goes. She goes to the oeil-de-boeuf window, unlatches it, swings it out and open, leans out and shouts)* Hey! Up here! *(She takes some keys from the windowsill and throws them into the alley)* Catch... It's the red one... Got it?

SHORT PAUSE. (KATE shuts the window and returns to her place on the sofa)

(There is knocking on door stage right off. KATE in a light voice) Come in. *(Knocking again. Annoyed, she bellows)* It's open!

(DJ staggers into the flat, breathless)

Welcome.

(DJ nods)

You found us.

(DJ nods)

What's wrong with you? Out of breath?

(DJ nods his head 'yes')

You can't smoke here. If that's what it is... If you're a smoker?...

SHORT PAUSE

Catch your breath then.

SHORT PAUSE

Where's the key? *(DJ holds up the key. She takes the key from him and hangs it on a hook in the window frame)* Don't want to lose it. I'd spend time and money getting it replaced—and I have precious little of either...

SHORT PAUSE

(DJ is looking at a painting on the wall. He puts on a pair of eyeglasses to examine the painting closely) I'm sorry, it's dark. It's also cold. And damp. I'd offer to take your coat but you'll want to keep it on. Welcome to winter in Shanghai. I'm accustomed to it. A lot like winter in Paris. Rain, damp, cold. You know Paris? *(DJ is looking at a piece of furniture near the dog's bed)* Mind the dog. *(DJ turns and looks at KATE)* Ruby. She's sleeping. She likes the blanket over her. Eleven years old now. Probably my last dog. *(DJ looks over the bookshelves)* My books are going to the Hoover Institute. Stanford University. California. I've read all of them... Some twice.

SHORT PAUSE

Enough about me. Who *are* you?

DJ: I met David Carlson in Beijing. He said I should meet you. He said you knew Shanghai better than anyone alive.

KATE: Carlson? Oh, yes... I got a fax... You're a writer.

DJ: Yes.

KATE: A journalist?

DJ: No. I'm not a journalist. I make my living writing non-fiction. Books on China. Hong Kong... Asia.

KATE: Travel books?

DJ: I'll write anything they pay me to write.

KATE: Freelance... Don't envy you... You make any money?

DJ: Never enough. But it's good work.

           SHORT PAUSE

KATE: Do you like dogs?

DJ: Yes. *(He points at Ruby's bed)* Is it friendly?

KATE: She. Her. Yes, most of the time... *(She watches DJ approach the dog)* 'Course, she doesn't like men...

DJ: Oh. *(He reaches out cautiously and pets the blanket)*

KATE: She likes you... Isn't that a kick?

           SHORT PAUSE

I'm not a writer... I don't pretend to be a writer. I came to it too late... Like Chinese. I started learning the language when I was 49. A disaster...

DJ: You've produced some wonderful books. I have all of them. Except one.

KATE: Which one?

DJ: *Frenchtown.*

KATE: You want *Frenchtown?*

DJ: Please.

KATE: It's 40 U.S. Three-fifty koi. *(She digs into her pockets)* I've got change... But I'm not a writer... Now, if you want to pay cash—U.S dollar cash—I'll do something on the price. How's 35?

DJ: Great. *(He digs into his pocket. He gives her the money. She retrieves the book from a box amongst a stack of boxes of books piled against the wall)*

KATE: Architecture is my thing. My passion... Truth be told, I write captions—that's all. Captions to pictures. Most of the buildings in that book are now gone.

DJ: Gone?

KATE: Demolished. For the almighty dollar. Or the raging renminbi... Shanghai *is* the culture of commerce. That's its politics. The only place that seems safe from the wrecker's ball is the Bund. The riverfront. The old bank buildings. The hongs... They say they want to preserve it. That's what they say. 'Course, for the right price they'll say whatever you want—and sell you whatever you want. It's all capitalist rubbish to them. They've got 5,000 years of history—what do they care for a piffling century of colonial architecture?... They've got a point, you know. Why should they care? *(The phone rings once. KATE picks it up)* Wei? *(She listens. A BRIEF PAUSE and then she hangs up. She stares at the phone and then picks up the receiver again. She listens. She hangs it up again)* Nothing. Not even a wrong number— just nothing. Silence...

          SILENCE

          Coffee?

DJ: Yes... Thank you.

KATE: It'll be instant.... I don't cook...

DJ: Fine with me...

KATE: Black?

DJ: Please.

                   *(KATE exits. The heater comes on in the room. DJ looks up
                   at the fluttering red ribbons. We hear KATE speaking
                   Chinese to CAT off stage. KATE re-enters)*

KATE: Heat.

DJ: Yes.

KATE: At least that's what the landlord calls it.

                   SHORT PAUSE

                   How long are you staying?

DJ: I don't know.

KATE: What, a week, a month, years?

DJ: A couple of months... I've got some time.

KATE: Your first time in Shanghai?

DJ: No.

KATE: Where are you staying?

DJ: It's a hotel. It's also part of a sports stadium. It's diffi-
             cult to explain.

KATE: The new Shanghai... I know a couple of lovely little
             guest houses. Resting places for the cadres. If you're
             interested? Not too pricey... I'm tight. Very tight with
             my money. I'd never send you somewhere pricey, or
             grand. But clean. Clean and reasonable.

DJ: What about a flat? Is it possible?

KATE: Yes. It's possible.

DJ: *(DJ points at the floor in front of a chair)* Do you mind?

KATE: Mind what?

DJ: I have a bad back. Could I lie on the floor a minute? It
             helps...

KATE: Sure... It's filthy. But go ahead...

DJ: I broke it in India. *(He lies down on the floor in front of the
             chair. He kicks off his shoes and rests his feet on the seat of the
             chair)* My back and my foot.

KATE: Both? At the same time?

DJ: Yes.

KATE: I won't ask how.

DJ: I was tired.

KATE: Drunk? Is that what you mean?

DJ: No. It was late. I was brushing my teeth. The floor was
               wet. I turned to reach for a towel and my feet went
               out from under me. My right foot hit the pipes
               under the sink. My fifth lumbar vertebra struck the
               toilet bowl. My head hit the tub... I crawled back to
               my bed and tried to sleep. I thought I could sleep
               through it: I'd wake up and it would all be over. I'd be
               better. Restored.

               *(CAT enters carrying a cup of coffee. She stops and stands in
               the middle of the room. CAT is KATE's ayee or maid)*

CAT: Excuse me. Where will you drink your coffee?

KATE: This is Cat. My ayee. She's here a few hours every day.
               Keeps things in order. Runs errands. Walks Ruby when
               I'm busy.

DJ: Hello.

CAT: Hello. Your coffee? Where shall I put it?

DJ: It doesn't matter... Thanks.

              (PAUSE as CAT considers his response. She then kneels and places the cup and saucer of coffee on the floor at her feet. She rises then looks down at him)

CAT: It's hot.

              (CAT exits. DJ looks at the cup and saucer in the middle of the floor and then looks across at KATE)

KATE: She doesn't get your meaning.

DJ: What part of it?

KATE: The 'it doesn't matter'. You confused her. Too much choice. She was waiting for instruction. You have to be precise. Literal, not literary.

DJ: Her English is very good.

KATE: Comes from Anhui Province. Don't know much about her. Seems honest. Has a young son about 10. Husband dead. Sometimes you don't want to know too much about them. Too many sad stories... It's changed. It's better—getting better every day... You're not here to write about the new China are you?

DJ: No. *(DJ rises, retrieves the cup and saucer of coffee. Sits in the chair and drinks the coffee)*

KATE: The Cultural Revolution?

DJ: No.

KATE: Sightseeing? Is that the plan?

DJ: There is one thing I want to do. And I've been told you're about the only person who might just be able to help me. *(He reaches into his coat pocket and pulls out his wallet. He opens his wallet and slides out a small black and white photograph. He holds it up to KATE. She puts on her glasses and crosses the room to take it from him. KATE squints at the photo)* It's my mother's house. The first home she knew. *(SHORT PAUSE)* I started carrying the photograph in my wallet when my grandfather died. Five years ago. I thought some day I'll go and find that house... He worked for Mackenzie & Company. He spoke Mandarin, Japanese and some Korean...

KATE: What year was she born?

DJ: 1926.

KATE: Family name?

DJ: Twilley.

KATE: Address?

DJ: Rue Amiral Courbet.

KATE: All the street names have changed.

DJ: I know.

(KATE exits. She is completely absorbed by the photograph. SILENCE. DJ stands, moves toward Ruby's bed. He kneels, makes a kissing sound as if to draw the dog out from under its covers. CAT enters. She watches him for a moment)

CAT: Would you like some more coffee?

DJ: No, thank you... Where did you learn your English?

CAT: American movies.

(KATE enters carrying a Shanghai telephone directory from 1930)

KATE: Here it is. Rue Amiral Courbet. It's now Fumin Lu.

DJ: They're in the book?

KATE: *(She hands him the telephone directory)* Yup. Right here. I'm pretty sure it's still there. At least it was a couple of weeks ago.

DJ: *(Referring to directory)* Where did you find this?

KATE: Flea market. There are all kinds of them. Sprout-ing up like weeds. If you're lucky you can dig up a treasure... I have... I do...

DJ: How long have you been in Shanghai?

KATE: I was posted to the U.S. Consulate in the early '80s. Then they posted me to Paris. I hated Paris... Then there was Tiananmen. No one wanted to be in China after June 4. Didn't bother me... First chance I had I asked to be sent back. It was dead here. Dead... I did-n't care. I love China. I'll never leave. Ever...

             (CAT exits. KATE watches her exit)

             SHORT PAUSE

             Are you married?

DJ: What?

KATE: Are you married?

DJ: No.

KATE: Not married?

DJ: No.

KATE: Divorced?

DJ: No.

KATE: Not married. Not divorced.

DJ: No.

KATE: Middle-aged.

DJ: I suppose. Yes.

KATE: Single middle-aged male.

DJ: Yes. It happens.

KATE: Not often... You're bright. Good looking... Do you drink?

DJ: I used to.

KATE: (*As if this explained everything*) Ohhh...

DJ: I was never violent. Just drunk.

KATE: None of my business what you are.

DJ: It was a long time ago.

KATE: Well, you're a catch. That's what I'm saying. A catch...
           And every single girl in Shanghai will be out to snag
           you.

DJ: I'll be careful...

KATE: Yes, you do that...

           (CAT enters. She moves to retrieve DJ's coffee cup and
           saucer)

           Tiananmen scared the Chinese more than it scared
           anyone else. They want out before it happens again.

DJ: (To CAT) Is that what you want?

CAT: What?

DJ: To get out?

           LONG PAUSE. (CAT exits quickly)

           What did I do?

KATE: No matter what she feels about her life here she is
             still—and always will be—Chinese. Do not ask her to
             go against that.

DJ: I wasn't suggesting treason.

KATE: Sounded like treason to me... Spiritual treason, but
             treason just the same.

DJ: What's her story?

KATE: She and her son share a room. Very bright but few
             prospects... Not long ago you needed permission to
             travel. The laws are changing, or not being enforced, so
             you've got this great migration to the cities. Millions
             on the move for a better life...

DJ: How old is she?

KATE: Twenty-eight. At least that's what she says.

DJ: Did I insult her?

KATE: No. Maybe. I don't know.

DJ: But I might have?

KATE: You might have.

DJ: Should I apologize?

KATE: If you apologize she'll know you insulted her... If she
               wasn't sure before, she'll be sure now and then you'll
               never get out of it.

DJ: What do I do?

KATE: Wait.

DJ: Wait?

KATE: Yeah. For a while. Then forget about it. Drop it. This
               is China. If you don't learn fast to drop misapprehen-
               sions they'll overwhelm you. You'll get stuck in them.
               Drop it. Get on with it. Forget about it... *(SHORT
               PAUSE)* I'll draw you a map.

DJ: What?

KATE: To your mother's house. It's not far. You just follow
               Hwei Hai Lu until it forks. Near Donghu Lu. I think.
               'Course it's changed in 60 years. Won't look quite like
               your photo. *(KATE sits at her desk and begins to draw out
               the map)* It's just up from the Donghu Lu Guesthouse.
               Nice little compound—mostly out of town cadres—
               but your dollar's always welcome.

DJ: One last thing.

KATE: You're not going to ask to borrow money are you?

DJ: Does that happen a lot?

KATE: Oh, all the time. Students mostly. Lost little souls far
               away from home and Daddy's deep pockets.

DJ: No. I'm not going to ask for money.

KATE: No. No, you're not really the type, are you? A little too
               old for that... Still, you never know how anyone's fixed.
               Right? Never judge a book... Right?

DJ: Actually, I was wondering if you'd autograph your book
               for me. *Frenchtown.*

               (KATE is hugely flattered. She blushes)

KATE: I don't do signings, you know. I don't go around sign-
               ing books. I'm not an *author,* if you know what I mean.

DJ: I'd really appreciate it.

KATE: Well, alright...

DJ: Great. *(He opens the book on the desk in front of her. KATE
               begins rummaging through the top drawer of her desk)* I
               have a pen.

KATE: No, I've got a special one I use... The paper's glossy.
           Not all pens work. Here it is. *(She pulls out the pen. She
           uncaps it)* So. What should I say?

DJ: Well—

KATE: —Wait. *(She thinks a moment)* I know... *(KATE begins to
           write an inscription)*

           BLACKOUT

ACT I, SCENE II

One week later.

The walled garden at the back of KATE's home in the old French Concession. The walls are six feet high. Patches of stucco have fallen off revealing dark red bricks underneath. The stucco is light grey. Pieces of broken Coca-Cola bottles have been cemented along the top of the wall. There is a door leading out of the garden upstage facing the audience. The door gives onto a back alley.

There are a few rose bushes and one or two small, skeletal, leafless trees. The grass is thin and short. There are two wood lawn chairs upstage left facing the audience. A small table sits between them.

KATE and DJ are sitting in the lawn chairs. They have been drinking Chinese tea. A small teapot and three covered cups sit on the table between the two garden chairs. KATE has a cardboard box on her lap. The box contains cups and bowls and figurines of blue and white porcelain. KATE is searching for something of interest. She picks out a small tea cup.

> *PAUSE as KATE examines the tea cup.*

KATE: *(She holds up the cup for DJ to see)* Ching Dynasty...

DJ: Beautiful.

KATE: *Early* Ching.

DJ: Where did you find it?

KATE: Every once in a while a friend comes by with a box of
                       whatever. Lets me choose what I want. Gives me a
                       price. A good price. Or so he says... Sometimes there's
                       a gem. Mostly it's junk.

DJ: What's the verdict?

KATE: This one's good... The rest... Mostly it's junk. Fakes.
                       But good fakes.

DJ: They're making fake antiques?

KATE: They've been making fakes in China for centuries...
                       This is a recent fake. Maybe a hundred years old. An
                       antique fake. But a good one.

DJ: It's beautiful...

                       SHORT PAUSE. (KATE is examining the cup)

KATE: Two hundred and fifty years is just a number. But if you
                       say this cup was made when George Washington was
                       President... Suddenly it has history, meaning and
                       value...

DJ: It's very simple... That's what I like...

KATE: America has jazz. China has blue and white porcelain…

DJ: Is it expensive?

KATE: The imperial stuff is pricey but the common stuff—
               something like this—is only a few dollars. If you can
               find it…

DJ: Can you get it out of the country?

KATE: Yes. No. Sometimes… A friend in Beijing had a big col-
               lection. He'd been in China for decades. He called the
               antiquities people. Three or four 'experts' showed up
               at his home. He had everything out on his dining room
               table. The head expert pointed to a vase and said, "No.
               That's not going anywhere. It's a national treasure." So
               my friend picked it up and smashed it on the floor.
               And then he said, "Is there anything else you'd like to
               keep in China?" They didn't know what to do. So they
               let him leave with everything… Barbaric… but effec-
               tive…

               *(There is a knock on the door to the alley. KATE rises and
               opens the door. HONGYONG stands in the doorway. He is
               wearing sunglasses and carries vegetables in a plastic bag)*

               Yes?

(HONGYONG holds out the bag of vegetables. KATE takes the bag. She opens it)

Bok Choy.

(She hands back the bag)

Upstairs.

(KATE shuts the door in HONGYONG's face)

DJ: Who was that?

KATE: His name is Hongyong. My ayee's son. Cat's son. You met Cat, remember?

DJ: Yes, we've met. Her son?

KATE: Father's dead. At least that's what she says.

DJ: Hong... Yong?

KATE: Hongyong. It means grand and courageous. Courageous, yes. Grand, well... Not so sure about that.

DJ: I was wondering where my sunglasses went.

KATE: They're yours?

DJ: I thought I'd lost them.

KATE: He didn't steal them. I'm sure he didn't steal them. He
                    must have found them.

DJ: It doesn't matter. I have another pair.

                    (There is a knock on the door to the alley)

KATE: That'll be Sam.

DJ: The journalist?

KATE: Yes.

DJ: His name's *Sam?*

KATE: He asked me to give him an English name. It's what
                    came to mind.

DJ: Right. *(He stands and faces the door; waiting for SAM to
                    enter)*

                    (There is another knock on the door)

KATE: Come in.

                    SHORT PAUSE. (Another knock)

Yes!

(The door opens slowly. SAM pokes his head in. KATE motions him to enter)

Come, come. Enter. Don't be shy.

SAM: I'm late. I'm sorry.

KATE: DJ—Sam; Sam—DJ.

SAM: How do you do? *(He offers his hand to DJ; they shake hands)*

DJ: How are you?

SAM: Fine. Thank you.

DJ: You're a journalist?

SAM: Yes.

DJ: Who do you write for?

SAM: *Xinhua*.

DJ: That's a government publication?

SAM: In China, they're all government publications.

DJ: Right.

SAM: But it's changing.

DJ: Is it?

SAM: Yes... And you? Who do you write for?

DJ: I'm freelance. I write for whoever wants to pay me... If
               they *pay* me I'll do it. Whatever it is. Freelance. That's
               what it means.

SAM: I know what it means.

DJ: Yes. Your English is impeccable.

SAM: I have an education. Even in China we study. I studied
               (counts off the subjects with his fingers) history, geography,
               mathematics, philosophy and science.

DJ: And English.

SAM: Yes. And English.

               SHORT PAUSE

KATE: *(To SAM)* Tea?

SAM: Yes, please.

(KATE pours him some tea)

KATE: *(To DJ)* Top you up?

DJ: Thanks. *(KATE tops up his tea)*

                 SHORT PAUSE. (They sip their tea)

                 My grandfather did that.

SAM: What?

DJ: Count. Like that: one, two, three, four, five. *(DJ demonstrates by counting to five with the thumb and finger of one hand. People from the West tend to count by opening their hand one finger at a time. Chinese people—even those who have lived in the West for many years—count by closing the hand. DJ counts one by placing the thumb across the palm. Number two is signified by placing the index finger across the thumb. Three is the middle finger placed over the thumb. Four and five follow this pattern)* I remember when I was very young noticing that he counted this way—by closing his hand rather than by opening it. I didn't understand until I arrived in China. In China everyone counts like that...

SAM: And how do you count in the West?

DJ:	We open our hand. Like this. *(He makes a fist and then counts off as he opens his hand:)* One, two, three, four, five.
KATE:	Isn't that a kick?
DJ:	Kate says that you know what's really happening in China. Do you?
SAM:	No.
KATE:	Good answer.
SAM:	It's the only answer.
DJ:	How did you meet?
SAM:	I was researching a story about U.S. visa applications. I met Kate at the Consulate. I interviewed her for the story.
KATE:	I'm often the first American they meet. I advise them on visa applications. I lend a hand.
DJ:	Are lots of people trying to get out?
SAM:	Not everyone wants to leave China... I don't want to leave. My wife does not want to leave. And my son will not leave. We believe in China.

DJ: Have you spent any time in the West?

SAM: Yes. I was posted to London for a while. I liked it. But
             I like China more.

KATE: He's a believer.

SAM: And what brought you to China?

DJ: Work... Work brought me here. Work keeps me here.
             It's hard to make a living as a writer in the West. It's
             easier here. At least there's less competition. And
             one project seems to lead to the next... And there's a
             family connection. My mother was born in Shanghai.

SAM: Foreigners move to China for two reasons. They have
             Chinese expertise Western companies value, or they
             have Western expertise Chinese companies value.

KATE: The only expertise that counts in China is survival.
             Get that right and you'll do just fine.

DJ: I never wanted to come East. I'd heard so much about
             it when I was a child. It didn't interest me. But when I
             got here I fell in love with it.

KATE: They say if you stay a week you'll write a book. If you
             stay a month you'll write an essay. And if you stay a year
             you'll send a postcard home.

DJ: The more you know the less you see.

                       *(A plastic bag is thrown over the wall into the garden.
                       KATE picks up the bag and opens it)*

                       He's shopping.

KATE: I better let him in before he gets to the eggs.

                       *(KATE opens the door to the garden. She steps into the alley
                       and looks right and then left. She sees HONGYONG and
                       motions for him to come to her)*

                       Come... Come in.

                       (HONGYONG enters. He wears sunglasses)

                       He's waiting for his mother.

DJ: Does he go to school?

KATE: Of course he goes to school.

DJ: How's his English?

KATE: *(To HONGYONG)* How's your English?

                       *(HONGYONG raises his middle finger to her. He sits in one
                       of the lawn chairs)*

DJ: Expressive.

SAM: Appalling...

KATE: He didn't learn that in school.

DJ: No?

SAM: American films.

KATE: That's right. Blame the Yanks.

DJ: I learned about China from my grandfather's stories...
                One day he was walking in the country with a friend...
                A Chinese friend... They're walking by a canal. Up
                ahead they see a young girl in the water. She's drown-
                ing. A crowd's gathered at the edge of the canal. No
                one's making any effort to save the girl. My grandfather
                begins stripping off his clothes. His friend tackles him.
                He holds him down. He won't let him save the girl. She
                drowns. My grandfather's friend explains that if he'd
                saved the girl he'd become responsible for her life. She
                would become *his* child...

SAM: Would they have saved her if she was white? I think
                they would have saved her if she was white...

DJ: Perhaps.

SAM: Are you married?

DJ: No.

              SHORT PAUSE

KATE: I prefer a dog.

DJ: Dogs are good.

              (KATE points to one of the rose bushes)

KATE: That's Sammy... Over there, the yellow rose bush...
              that's Hillary.

SAM: Your dogs?

KATE: Yes... Both of them... Keeps them close.

DJ: I thought dogs were a bourgeois thing.

KATE: They are. Unless you buy a licence. If you buy a licence
              they're something else entirely.

DJ: What?

KATE: Acceptable.

DJ: Is it expensive?

KATE: Probably.

DJ: You don't have a licence?

KATE: If I apply for a licence they might say no. If they say no
               I'll have to put her down or leave. Neither option is
               particularly appealing... In China it's not so much that
               you need them to say yes, you just don't want them to
               say no...

               *(HONGYONG stands. He turns and moves upstage. He
               stands in front of the backstage wall of the garden, his back to
               the audience. He unzips his fly and urinates against the back
               wall of the garden)*

               Sorry.

DJ: It could be worse...

SAM: What would your family do if you married a Chinese
               woman?

DJ: I don't know.

SAM: How would they feel?

DJ: I don't have anything to do with them. Except through
               lawyers... I haven't spoken to any of them in over 10
               years.

KATE: Sex, money or politics?

DJ: I joined the family firm.

KATE: Oh... All three! Well done!

SAM: You haven't had any contact with your family in 10 years?

KATE: When you get rich you'll understand.

SAM: When I'm rich?

KATE: Yes... When your unhappiness is no longer blamed on poverty and the lack of opportunity.

SAM: I'm not unhappy.

KATE: Oh yes you are. You just haven't had the time to notice.

SHORT PAUSE

DJ: *(To SAM)* I went to work for my father. It was a mistake. It ended badly.

SAM: Your father has a business? You're very lucky.

DJ: Not so lucky... I always thought he was something spe-
                    cial. But he's weak and vain and not very smart... He's
                    a very *ordinary* man.

SAM: I don't understand.

DJ: It's a long story.

                    *(HONGYONG moves toward the door. He stops and turns
                    and looks at KATE)*

                    He's bored.

                    *(HONGYONG goes to KATE and offers his hand. KATE
                    shakes his hand)*

KATE: Good-bye.

                    *(HONGYONG goes to SAM and offers his hand. SAM
                    shakes his hand)*

SAM: Goodbye.

                    *(HONGYONG goes to DJ and offers his hand. DJ shakes
                    his hand)*

DJ: Goodbye.

(DJ holds onto HONGYONG's hand. HONGYONG tries to pull his hand free. DJ smiles)

Can you swim?

(HONGYONG stops struggling to break free)

HONGYONG: Can you?

(DJ releases HONGYONG's hand. HONGYONG turns and exits, shutting the door behind him)

BLACKOUT

ACT I, SCENE III

DJ's flat in a new high rise in what was the French Concession. In Shanghai, flats are sold unfinished; essentially, you buy a space with bare concrete walls. Often a second contractor is hired to 'outfit' the flat—finish the bathrooms, install the lighting and lay whatever flooring you might choose. DJ has rented a flat that is not fully finished. To someone from the West it has the look and feel of a loft—which is why DJ feels comfortable in the space. A native Chinese would not live in it as it is.

There is a sofa and chair covered in white sheets. The rest of the flat is empty. There are doors leading off to the kitchen, bedrooms and bathroom. There is the sound of a key in the front door upstage. The door shakes. Finally, the door opens. DJ and CAT enter. DJ and CAT enter slowly. They begin silently exploring the space. They open and shut doors leading off. They both explore the space for different reasons. He wants to see if it will serve his needs. She explores it as if it were a new planet—something she can't quite believe exists.

DJ: What do you think?

CAT: It's big.

DJ: Is it too much for you?

CAT: Too much?

DJ: Too big a job.

CAT: No. It's a big flat for only one person.

DJ: Are you sure you can do it?... Kate keeps you pretty
                busy.

CAT: Will you pay me?

DJ: Yes.

CAT: If you pay me I'll do the work.

DJ: Good.

CAT: Cash.

DJ: What?

CAT: You pay me cash.

DJ: Yes, of course.

CAT: I come once a week and you pay me 800 koi a month.
                And that's just for cleaning... No extras.

DJ: Extras?

CAT: I do extras for Kate. Sometimes I do windows. Some-
                times I iron clothes.

DJ: Oh. Right. Extras... So, a hundred U.S.?... Yes, that's
                fine...

CAT: I can do it.

DJ: I'm sure you can.

CAT: It's not as if there's a lot to do. I mean, there's not much here to clean. Is there?

DJ: Dusting. Cleaning.

CAT: Bathroom? Kitchen?

DJ: Yes.

CAT: Good. That's okay...

DJ: I really don't know how long I'm going to stay.

CAT: You said three months.

DJ: Yes. I've agreed to take the flat for three months. A minimum of three months. So, yes, I'll be here three months anyway.

CAT: I'll start now.

DJ: Right now?

CAT: Yes.

DJ: You don't have to.

CAT: I want to.

DJ: Can I help?

CAT: Help?

DJ: It's a big job.

CAT: I can do it.

DJ: I know.

           SHORT PAUSE.

CAT: I need some money. There's nothing here. I need to
           buy some soap, a mop and a broom... There's nothing
           here.

DJ: How much do you need?

CAT: Two hundred koi.

           *SHORT PAUSE. (DJ searches through his pockets for the
           money)*

DJ: It's just the two of you?

CAT: What?

DJ: You and your son?

CAT: Yes.

                SHORT PAUSE

DJ: Where were you born?

CAT: In the country.

DJ: Where?

CAT: A small village.

                (DJ hands her the money. He watches as she counts it)

DJ: What's the name of your village?

CAT: It's too small. It's not even on the map.

DJ: But what's it called?

CAT: Taiyuan.

DJ: Ty-yung?

CAT: Tie-yun.

SHORT PAUSE

DJ: Well?

CAT: Well what?

DJ: Is it correct? The money?

CAT: Yes. Yes, it's correct.

SHORT PAUSE

DJ: Your English is very good.

CAT: I learned to speak it from the movies... When I was young I would label everything in the house with its English name: the chair, the table, the window. I labelled everything... No one else worked as hard at English as I did.

SHORT PAUSE

           How old are you?

DJ: Forty-two.

CAT: Oh.

DJ: Oh? What does that mean? *Oh...*

CAT: You are very old.

DJ: Thanks.

CAT: You are much older than I thought.

DJ: Really? How old did you think I was?

CAT: I don't know. But I didn't think you were 42...

DJ: I don't *feel* old.

           PAUSE

CAT: Have you ever been in love?

DJ: That's a very personal question.

CAT: Yes, I know.

           SHORT PAUSE

DJ: Yes, I've been in love.

CAT: Love is different than sex.

DJ: Yes... It is...

           SHORT PAUSE

CAT: Why didn't you get married?

DJ: It wasn't what I wanted.

CAT: But you had sex?

DJ: Yes

CAT: Did you like it?

DJ: Yes, I liked it.

CAT: Then why didn't you get married?

DJ: It wouldn't have worked.

CAT: Did she like to have sex with you?

DJ: Yes. I think so.

CAT: What did she like about it?

DJ: You'd have to ask her...

CAT: To me, sex means children or disease.

DJ: It's a bit more than that.

CAT: Is it?

DJ: It can be.

CAT: Tell me...

DJ: I'm really not the best person to ask.

CAT: Do you like Chinese women?

DJ: Yes.

CAT: Why do you like Chinese women?

DJ: I don't know. Because they're different.

CAT: How are they different?

DJ: It's complicated...

CAT: Many Chinese women would like to marry a man from
           the West. They think it will make them rich and free.

DJ: Is that what you want?

CAT: Of course. Everybody wants to be rich and free.

DJ: I think it's overrated.

CAT: Do you?

DJ: Yes...

SHORT PAUSE

Taiyuan?

CAT: *(She nods yes)* Taiyuan... Your accent is very good.

DJ: The capital of Shanxi Province. A big city. Four million people?...Why did you say you were from Taiyuan? It's not a village. Is it? Nowhere close.

CAT: No...

DJ: Why did you lie?

CAT: I don't know.

DJ: Are you trying to hide something?

CAT: No.

DJ: Don't play with me.

CAT: I'm not playing.

SHORT PAUSE

DJ: Listen... I don't *want* you...

(CAT smiles)

I'm serious.

CAT: Wait till you see how hard I work.

DJ: I'm sure you work very hard.

CAT: No one works harder...

DJ: What I mean is I don't want to sleep with you. I don't want to have sex with you—not that you aren't very attractive—of course you are. But that's not what I want.

CAT: What do you want?

DJ: A housekeeper.

CAT: That's all?

DJ: Yes.

CAT: Men want sex.

DJ: I don't want sex.

CAT: Do you think I'm pretty?

DJ: Yes, you're a very pretty girl.

CAT: Everybody wants something.

DJ: I'm not sure what I want. Not really. Maybe wanting something and never getting it is normal. Maybe that's just how we're supposed to live—always left wanting.

             SHORT PAUSE

DJ: Why are you smiling?

CAT: You were angry.

DJ: You lied to me. About your village. Where you came from. It made me angry.

CAT: You are a different man when you're angry.

             PAUSE

             I'm not a prostitute.

DJ: I know...

             SHORT PAUSE

CAT: There's something else.

DJ: What?

CAT: I need a key. Will you give me a key?

DJ: Oh... Yes.

CAT: My own key?

DJ: Yes. Yours.

CAT: I can come and go as I please?

DJ: Sure. Any time.

               *(CAT sits down on the sofa) SHORT PAUSE. (She looks up
               at DJ. DJ's back is to the audience)*

CAT: Sit down... Sit down beside me. I want to know more
               about you...

DJ: Why?

CAT: Maybe I can help you.

DJ: How?

CAT: Maybe I can help you find what you are looking for.

DJ: But I don't know what I'm looking for.

CAT: So I'll help you.

DJ: Now I'm frightened.

CAT: Are you?

DJ: *(Smiling)* Yes... Terrified...

            SILENCE

            BLACKOUT

ACT I, SCENE IV

KATE's flat. KATE and JAMES are drinking martinis. JAMES is in his late 70s. He is short and heavy-set.

KATE: All sorts of people track me down for all sorts of reasons... Usually, it's because they were born here and want to find the family home... Is that what you're after?

JAMES: No...

KATE: What then?

JAMES: Have you lived here a long time?

KATE: Here? This flat?

JAMES: Shanghai.

KATE: Off and on for about 15 years... Mostly on.

JAMES: Don't you miss the States?

KATE: Some parts of it... But if I moved back I'd be just another old lady on the veranda. Here, I have a purpose. As I say, people come to me, they seek me out. I have something they're looking for... I'm popular... I always wanted to be popular. *(She laughs at her joke)*

JAMES: I'm sure you are.

KATE: Top you up?

JAMES: What?

KATE: A splash more?

JAMES: Lovely... I'm not really much of a cocktail drinker. Scotch is my drink. *(She fills his glass)* Thank you.

KATE: How long are you staying?

JAMES: Don't know. A couple of weeks... I've got nothing to run back to, if that's what you mean.

KATE: I was an only child... And a late unexpected child. I think they had resigned themselves to being childless. And then I came along... My mother was 45 when I was born... Imagine the surprise... They were settled. Mature. Prosperous. Not like all the other families— the young families struggling... I remember the first thing that struck me about other people's families was the noise. At the dinner table. I could hardly think... At my home, at my parents' table it was silent. Not that we didn't speak, we just didn't speak over each other. We didn't shout... A Tiffany chandelier hung over the table... Luminous... A grandfather clock against the wall. Ticking. Marking the quarter hour, half hour and on the hour. And our voices. Speaking without tension. Speaking without being in a hurry to get somewhere... And the *diction*... God, the *diction*...

JAMES: I know what you mean.

KATE: Do you?... Do you really?

JAMES: I *eat* alone. Since my wife died. I eat alone. I have the television... sometimes... as company. No clock, no *grandfather* clock. My parents had one. I never did.

PAUSE

KATE: No... I won't leave China. Not as long as I'm healthy... People are always after me for something—looking for a family home. Tracing old memories... Walking tours...

JAMES: What?

KATE: I do walking tours... I take people through the French Concession—point out the sites... What's left, anyway...

JAMES: You charge money for this?

KATE: Yes. Oh yes.

JAMES: Cash money?

KATE: Yup.

JAMES: How much?

KATE: Why?

JAMES: You know, I said to myself—as I looked out over the rooftops from my hotel room, the 27th floor—I said to myself this is a land of opportunity... Isn't it?

KATE: Whatever do you mean?

JAMES: A land of opportunity... With the right introductions, with the correct approach, this is the time and place for commerce... Everywhere you look there's opportunity... Am I right?

KATE: It's China... It has always been thus...

JAMES: Eh?

KATE: *(She shouts as he seems hard of hearing)* It's China!

JAMES: Yes?

KATE: Well, yes, there's opportunity. But it's complicated.

JAMES: You get by? You make a good dollar?

KATE: Yes.

JAMES: You survive?

KATE: Yes, well, I have my walking tours. I sell my books. I lecture... but that's not serious money. If you want to make serious money you have to move into antiques... Source the opportunities. Exploit them.

JAMES: Now that's exciting.

KATE: I wouldn't call it exciting.

JAMES: No? What then?

KATE: Challenging.

JAMES: Still?

KATE: Yes. Well, I do come across the odd... I do make discoveries. Import/export of a higher order. Slip it out amongst the toiletries. No harm done.

JAMES: Yes, you see, that's what I'm talking about.

KATE: Keeps me flush.

JAMES: Dangerous?

KATE: Yes. Can be.

JAMES: Serious penalties?

KATE: Jail.

JAMES: Still?

KATE: Yes. Possible.

JAMES: I'm an entrepreneur... That's what I'm saying.

KATE: There you go...

JAMES: Museums don't interest me... Commerce interests me...

KATE: Yes?

JAMES: We'll talk?

KATE: Yes, we could.

JAMES: Import/export?

KATE: Yes. If you have the courage, the nerve to sneak it out.

JAMES: I'm an old man. Who's going to bother with an old man?

KATE: Yes, it's possible.

           PAUSE

JAMES: Could I use your washroom? *(He rises)*

KATE: Beijing belly? Gotta be careful where you eat. And what you eat... What you *choose*.

JAMES: *Plumbing*... Prostate... You know?

KATE: Oh dear.

JAMES: Yes. Annoying as hell. Sudden *urges*. Middle of the night.

KATE: What about surgery?

JAMES: A last resort. Yes. Sure. But the *consequences*... Don't ask me to go there... May I?

KATE: New medicines all the time. You've tried medication? You've got a good doctor? Have you?... God, not cancer. Is it cancer?

JAMES: No.

KATE: A fight. Isn't it? Old age. Everything goes wrong... I just want to drop dead. Just keel over.

JAMES: Excuse me...

KATE: Second on the left. Pink towel's for company. *(JAMES exits)* I think. *(She empties her glass)* Pink or blue. The clean one anyway. The clean one's for company... *(She picks the olive out of her glass and pops it into her mouth)* Last one... Last olive... No more. Saddest thing, a martini without an olive... Sans oleeve... Anymore slosh? *(She gets up and shakes martini shaker)* Oops, a splash. Just a splash... Don't mind if I do... *(She empties it into her glass)*

           SHORT PAUSE. (JAMES enters)

JAMES: ...Stew?

KATE: Pardon?

JAMES: I thought you said... ·

KATE: No... I said, 'What does your son do?'

JAMES: He's a writer.

KATE: What, a poet? A novelist? Tell me, what kind of writer is he?

JAMES:	It's not art. I don't think he'd call it art. He writes books.
KATE:	Writers are artists. I think. I think you'd call them artists. Most of them.
JAMES:	Well, he's not without some talent. That's for sure. I'd say he had talent... He had an audition. Once. He was ten. He loved music, always jumping around so my wife—it was her idea—she was the artistic one. She says let's take him to this audition... For a school... A dance school of all things... Like, ballet... Who knows, she says, maybe he's got talent. So we take him to the church hall. Full of parents and children. Middle of winter. Coats and boots, running noses, everything. You know? The works... He was 10, at the time... And so first thing is they have all the chldren—about 40 of them—stand up facing the teachers. The auditioners. Three of them sitting at a table facing the kids. The children. And the middle teacher says, "Okay, kids, I want you to pretend you're honey bees and buzz around like it's a sunny day and you're gathering honey..." 'So, off they go, all these little... Nothing special there, right. Everyone had a good laugh. Next she says, "Okay, I want you to pretend you're snowmen and you're melting... When I tell you, I want you to melt into puddles on the floor." So she says, "Off you go." And within about 20 seconds most of them had melted. Most of them were out on the floor. Puddles. But

in the middle of the room—standing there—was my son. He was melting, but melting in his own *sweet* time... One finger at a time... one eye, one appendage for Christ's sake... I kept wanting to say, "Come on, boy, melt for me. Get on with it. Stop making such a spectacle of yourself." I was so embarrassed. I mean, he was holding everything up with his melting—right?... So, finally it's done. He's melted. It's forgotten. And we're putting on our coats and the teacher—the auditioner—comes up to me and asks me if that's my son... The slow melter... I almost said no. Honestly, I almost said no. I was so embarrassed. I mean, how would you feel your son makes such a spectacle of himself? But she says no, he's brilliant and they want him. They want him and they'll even give him a scholarship. Can you believe it? Nuts. Just nuts... For melting?...

KATE: Did he take the scholarship?

JAMES: No. His mother had a change of heart. She was like that. She'd want something for him and then at the last moment she'd change course, take it away... What's that about anyway? ... Melting?

KATE: I'm out of olives...

JAMES: What?

KATE: Right clean out. No more.

JAMES: Should I run to the corner market?

KATE: There isn't one... I'll just nip out. A Dutch friend has a
            supply. I can't serve a martini without an olive, can I?
            What kind of a hostess is that?

JAMES: Should I come with you?

KATE: No. I won't be a minute. Be right back then.

JAMES: Do you really need them?

KATE: For the martinis.

JAMES: Forget the martinis. What about I take you to dinner?

KATE: Dinner?

JAMES: Let's make an evening out of it.

KATE: Oh my.

JAMES: I'm thinking steak... A porterhouse... Rare.

KATE: A porterhouse?...They wouldn't have a clue...

JAMES: They have beef, don't they? They gotta have beef.

KATE: Let me do another round... I'd love just one more...
             And I'm damned if I'm going to pay bar prices—you
             know? I'm cheap... Another round and we'll go looking
             for that steak.

JAMES: A porterhouse...

KATE: Yes... Won't be a minute... Now you've got me con-
             fused... My keys... No, you stay here, read a book,
             something... I'll just be a minute... No time at all...

JAMES: My good times know no bounds... I'm *renowned*... A
             night to *remember*... It'll be a *night* to remember...

KATE: You wait... Won't be a moment.

JAMES: I'll wait.

KATE: Good... Read something.

JAMES: Yes, I'll read...

             (KATE exits. JAMES looks around the flat. The heater
             comes on. Red ribbons flutter out on the heated air. JAMES
             sits on the sofa. He closes his eyes. He begins to snore)

             PAUSE

(HONGYONG appears outside the oeil-de-boeuf *window. He wears sunglasses. He has climbed down from the roof above. He pries open the window. He climbs in and drops down onto the floor. JAMES stops snoring. HONGYONG does not see JAMES on the sofa. JAMES wakes up. Ruby lets out a muffled bark from under her blankets. JAMES turns and sees HONGYONG. JAMES hides from HONGYONG's view. JAMES watches HONGYONG. HONGYONG goes to KATE's desk. He opens the top drawer. He reaches into his pant pocket to pull out some bills. He is about to put the money in KATE's drawer when JAMES speaks)*

JAMES: And what the hell are you up to?

SILENCE

English... *English?* Speak English? Fucking little thief. That's what you are.

(JAMES looks around the room for something with which to defend himself. There is a heavy walking stick by the front door. JAMES moves slowly toward the walking stick. He doesn't turn his back on HONGYONG or break eye contact)

I've got you now... You're done...

(JAMES picks up the walking stick. He stands up against the front door of the flat. He holds the stick with both hands as if it were a baseball bat)

Now, I'm not looking for trouble. I'm not. But if it's trouble you want you'll get it... First, I want you to... to put your hands up... Come on... Hands up!

(JAMES moves toward HONGYONG. HONGYONG backs into RUBY. RUBY lets out a muffled bark)

What's that? What's that you say?

(JAMES moves around in front of the desk. He holds the stick in both hands as if ready to strike at HONGYONG. HONGYONG moves back toward the window)

Alright... Alright... If you won't *surrender* then I'll chase you out the way you came. Ahh!

(JAMES swings the stick back and forth to scare HONG-YONG. HONGYONG laughs. JAMES stops and listens. He becomes angry)

Laugh at me? Laugh at *me*? I'll show you *funny*.

(JAMES raises the stick and moves toward HONGYONG. JAMES trips and falls to the ground. JAMES looks up at HONGYONG)

Now look what you've done.

(HONGYONG scrambles out the window. He cries out and slips and falls to the pavement one floor below. JAMES runs to the window and looks down at HONGYONG. He turns away from the window. He is shaken)

Oh, shit...

(JAMES takes out a handkerchief and mops his brow. He sits on the sofa to catch his breath. KATE appears at the front door. She is winded and frantic)

KATE: We need an ambulance. Hongyong's had a fall.

JAMES: Who?

KATE: My ayee's son. Little boy. Must have been trying to get in the window.

JAMES: He was robbing you. At your desk. Taking money.

KATE: I sent him on some errands. He was bringing back my change...

JAMES: Oh shit...

KATE: He's unconscious. *(She grabs a blanket from the sofa)* We need an ambulance.

PAUSE. (JAMES moves to the phone)

JAMES: *(Picking up the telephone receiver)* I'll call for an ambulance... Shall I?... Is it 911? Is that the emergency number here? 911? Or is it something else?... What is it? What's the number?

KATE: *(As she exits with the blanket)* He'll be going into shock.

JAMES: The number?... What's the number?

PAUSE

BLACKOUT

ACT II, SCENE I

Ten days later.

DJ's flat. DJ has decorated it sparsely but carefully. There is a table downstage centre. There are four chairs arranged around the table.

Everything in the flat is labelled. The name of each object is written in black ink on a coloured file card. Each card is taped to the object it names. This is to help HONGYONG learn English. It also refers to how CAT learned English.

DJ stands 12 feet from JAMES. JAMES is DJ's father. This is the first time they have met face to face in 10 years. JAMES watches DJ. He keeps a good distance between them. DJ avoids eye contact as much as possible.

SILENCE

DJ: How did you find me?

JAMES: From your books.

DJ: You *read* my books?

JAMES: I contacted the publishers. They weren't sure where you were. Then one wrote back saying they thought you were in Shanghai. They said there's this woman who knows all about Shanghai—a *resource* person. If you were here she'd know. They gave me her name. I tracked her down... I found you.

DJ: Kate...

JAMES: I asked her not to tell you. I told her I wanted it to be a surprise.

DJ: It's a surprise.

           PAUSE.

           You didn't *read* the books.

JAMES: Yes I did...

           PAUSE

DJ: So... You found me.

JAMES: Yes.

DJ: Why?

JAMES: Your mother's dead.

DJ: Yes, I know.

JAMES:	She asked me to find you.
DJ:	What? On her deathbed? "Please go find him and tell him…" Tell him what? What did she want you to tell me?
JAMES:	Nothing.
DJ:	But she wanted you to find me.
JAMES:	She made me promise.
DJ:	Why?
JAMES:	I don't know… She'd had a stroke. She couldn't speak well or think straight. She said things in riddles. Or at least they seemed like riddles. She didn't really say go find our *son*. She didn't say that. She didn't say make peace with him. She didn't get into any of that. But she did say, or seemed to say, find him.

(CAT enters)

JAMES:	Hello.
DJ:	Could you get us some tea? *(To JAMES)* You'll have some tea?

JAMES: Don't go to any trouble.

DJ: We'll have tea.

              (CAT exits)

              That's all she said? Or that's all she wanted?

JAMES: I had to try and make sense of it. It wasn't clear. All I
              know is that when I said I would find you it seemed to
              calm her. As if that's what she wanted to hear... I fig-
              ured I owed her that.

DJ: Where are you staying?

JAMES: *(Referring to CAT)* I know her...

DJ: Her name is Cat. You chased her son out a window.
              Remember?

JAMES: Is she your... *friend?*

DJ: She lives here with me. Her son lives here too.

JAMES: *Her* son?

DJ: Yes. He's 10. His name is Hongyong... It means grand
              and courageous.

JAMES: What does?

DJ: His name.

JAMES: Really? That's nice.

DJ: This *(indicating labels)* is Hongyong... These labels...
            The door, the chair, the table... He's learning English.

JAMES: How's his arm?

DJ: Getting better.

JAMES: Good.

            PAUSE

            Well... You look well.

DJ: I am.

JAMES: Is this *your* place?

DJ: I rent it.

JAMES: Have you been here long?

DJ: No. Not long.

JAMES: It's *unique*... isn't it?

DJ: It's how they sell flats here. Unfinished. I like it like
           this. Unfinished. It's like a loft... Sort of.

           (CAT enters with tea)

CAT: I made English tea. *(To JAMES)* What will you have in
           your tea?

JAMES: Milk and sugar.

CAT: One lump or two?

JAMES: Two. *(CAT prepares his tea)*

           (CAT is wearing a tight T-shirt. DJ notices)

DJ: What's that?

CAT: *(She hands JAMES his tea)* What?

DJ: On your shirt... You've spilled something.

CAT: No. I don't think so.

DJ: You have. Maybe you want to change into something
           else?

SHORT PAUSE. (They stare at each other. CAT under-
stands. DJ is suggesting that she is being flirtatious. She is
angry and exits quickly)

JAMES: She's *pretty*... She's a *pretty* girl.

DJ: She's not a girl, she's a woman. She's too old to be called
           a girl. At least in China... How long are you going to be
           in Shanghai?

JAMES: I don't know. I was thinking I might go on to Beijing...
           Since I'm here.

DJ: It's Bey-jing... like the jing in jingle. Bey-jing, not Beige-
           ing.

JAMES: Bey-jing.

DJ: It's a very different kind of city.

JAMES: Is it?

           (The doorbell buzzes. DJ ignores it. He pours himself a cup of
           tea. He drops a cube of sugar into his tea. He stirs the tea then
           taps the spoon loudly against the lip of the cup. The doorbell
           buzzes again)

           What's that?

DJ: Was I being rude? Tapping my spoon like that? Making too much noise?...

JAMES: No. I meant the door. The doorbell. It rang. Or buzzed.

DJ: The door?

JAMES: Aren't you going to answer it?

DJ: No...

JAMES: It could be important... Couldn't it?

DJ: Why don't you answer it?

JAMES: It's not my home.

DJ: No, it isn't, is it...

           (The door opens. KATE enters. She begins speaking almost immediately)

KATE: Hello! *(To JAMES)* Hello... Am I interrupting? Just wanted to drop off those books I mentioned.

JAMES: You're just in time for tea.

DJ: Yes, you are.

KATE: Am I?... *(To JAMES)* Hello again.

JAMES: Yes, hello.

DJ: We'll need another cup... Cat... Cat!

                  *(KATE hands DJ two books in a white plastic bag. DJ takes
                  the books out of the bag)*

KATE: Could I keep the bag? Unless you want it? *(DJ hands her
                  the bag. She stuffs the bag into her pocket. KATE explains to
                  JAMES)* Ruby. I never seem to have enough bags. You
                  know? You've got to pick it up. Even here.

DJ: In India they're a curse.

KATE: Dogs? Not dogs.

DJ: No. Plastic bags. They're everywhere. Like tumble-
                  weed... In Delhi... Recently.

KATE: *(To JAMES)* I never have enough of them. Always run-
                  ning out.

DJ: *(Shouting over KATE)* In Delhi!

84

(CAT enters. She wears a dressing gown over her clothes and very heavy rain boots)

CAT: Did you *call* me?

DJ: We need another cup.

CAT: A cup?

DJ: Yes. Another cup.

(CAT turns to exit)

Cat?

CAT: Yes.

DJ: Your shirt?

CAT: You were right... There was a stain... *(CAT turns to exit)*

DJ: Cat?

CAT: Yes?

DJ: Perhaps you could put on something else? Something more *appropriate?*...

(CAT is angry. She exits)

BRIEF PAUSE

DJ: *(As he delivers the speech he speaks faster and faster)*
             In Delhi, they did an autopsy on a cow. If that's the
             right word: autopsy. Anyway, the cow had died—one of
             their sacred cows... Wandering free. You know? And it
             had died and they were trying to find out why it had
             died. I guess in case it had a disease or something...
             They wanted to know what had killed it so they could
             stop it if it was contagious. So it wouldn't kill other
             cows... So... They opened it up. The dead cow. And
             they found it was full of plastic bags. It had been eat-
             ing plastic bags. It had 150 pounds of plastic in its
             stomach. That's what killed it. All those bags. Plugged
             it up. And the more plugged up it got the hungrier it
             got. The hungrier it got the more bags it ate. It looked
             like it had a full stomach. And it was full. I guess. But
             really it was starving to death... So the thing is they're
             trying to outlaw them.

KATE: Cows?

DJ: No. Plastic bags.

KATE: They're going to outlaw plastic bags?

DJ: Yes. That's what I read.

KATE: What will they replace them with?

DJ: Paper.

KATE: Paper bags?

DJ: Yes...

JAMES: What about the cows?

KATE: What about them?

JAMES: They're dying...

DJ: Yes?

JAMES: All those dead cows... Children starving...

DJ: They're *vegetarian*.

JAMES: Indians?

DJ: Hindus.

KATE: They eat fish.

JAMES: Hindus?

KATE: Yes... With their hands.

JAMES: My God... What a country!...

SHORT PAUSE

KATE: Necropsy.

DJ: What?

KATE: I remember. That's what it's called. Autopsy is humans. Necropsy is animals.

(CAT enters carrying a teacup and saucer. She has added a bright red scarf to her attire. DJ, KATE and JAMES watch her. She puts the cup and saucer down by the teapot. She picks up the teapot and turns to DJ)

CAT: More?

(DJ does not answer. CAT turns to KATE, she holds up the teapot)

KATE: Thank you. *(CAT pours tea)* That's fine. Thank you...

(CAT holds teapot up to JAMES)

JAMES: I'm good. Thank you... *(To CAT)* That's my son... I haven't seen him in ages. I tracked him down. It's a reunion. We're having a family reunion.

(CAT drops the teapot. It breaks into pieces. She exits quickly)

Oops-a-daisy... Oops...

PAUSE

(KATE begins picking up the pieces of the teapot. She puts the broken pieces into the plastic bag DJ returned to her. When she is finished she puts the plastic bag into a waste basket)

DJ: *(To KATE)* I don't know what he's doing here. I haven't seen him in 10 years... He says he's my father.

JAMES: I am.

DJ: It doesn't look like you.

JAMES: It's been a long time. I've aged. I'm an old man...

DJ: You're my father? I don't *see* my father... I haven't had a relationship of any kind with my father in over 10 years... Your clothes are too big. Do you know that? Are you aware of it? They don't fit. Have you lost weight?

JAMES: I'm old. You shrink.

DJ: The cuffs of your trousers drag on the floor. You stand
                on them. It's like you're wearing someone else's
                clothes... Are you sure you're my father?

KATE: Ten years is a long time...

JAMES: I brought you something. A silver box. Years ago, your
                mother put your name on it. Actually, she wrote your
                name and your grandfather's name. It was from him to
                you. He wanted you to have it and she wanted to be
                sure you got it. I brought it with me.

                *(JAMES takes a silver cigarette box out of his jacket pocket.
                He offers it to DJ. DJ takes it)*

KATE: What is it?

JAMES: It's silver.

KATE: What *is* it?

DJ: *(He opens the box and looks inside. He sees the piece of paper
                with his name written on it)* Yes, that's my name... I rec-
                ognize my mother's writing...

KATE: Can I see it?

DJ: It's a cigarette box... It was a wedding gift to my grand-
                father from his friend Bruno. There's his name:

B. Rische. And my grandfather's other German friends. All their names. They played lawn tennis together... And the date: November 18, 1925. The day my grandparents were married. At Trinity Cathedral in Shanghai.

JAMES: She wanted you to have it. Years ago, she said if anything happened to her to make sure you got it. So I brought it.

DJ: *(To KATE)* Bruno was a U-boat commander and the son of a Lutheran Bishop. He had First and Second Class Iron Crosses. My grandfather kept a photograph of Bruno on his dresser. I remember noticing it when I was very young. Bruno had a long scar running down one cheek from a sabre duel... If I hadn't seen the photograph and Bruno's name on this cigarette box I would have thought my grandfather had made him up... But you know, the older I get the more I see that he always told the truth. He didn't lie. He didn't make things up. He told the truth.

KATE: There was a big German community here between the Wars. Thirty thousand German Jews.

DJ: When my grandparents returned from their honeymoon in Hang Zhou they took a flat in a pension. Each resident had their own houseboy to serve tea and stoke the fire. Bruno moved into the flat across the hall.

KATE: What happened to Bruno?

DJ: I have to lie down...

KATE: Your back?

(DJ sits on the floor then stretches out on his back. He holds the silver box by his side).

DJ: My back.

JAMES: You have a bad back? I've got a bad back... Remember?

DJ: Bloody India... I've been everywhere everyone thinks they want to go: China, India, Africa, the Middle East—Afghanistan, for fuck's sake. The only place that scares me is India. I broke my back in Bombay. A few years later I got stuck in a bad monsoon. I picked up pneumonia. I almost died in Calcutta. I couldn't catch my breath. It was like being in the mountains. The air seemed so thin. Couldn't get enough of it into my lungs... All those other places nothing ever happened... Something about India... You don't *visit* India... You *survive* it...

SILENCE. PAUSE. (DJ is asleep)

KATE: That's it then... He's gone...

JAMES: Stress...

92

KATE: What?

JAMES: When he was a boy. Whenever something bad hap-
           pened, something unpleasant, he'd sleep... Stress re-
           action... That's what the doctor said... Stress...

KATE: We should probably go.

JAMES: The woman?

KATE: She'll be alright.

JAMES: Him?

KATE: He'll be fine.

JAMES: Good... He's my son, you know.

KATE: Yes. I know.

JAMES: I haven't seen him in years... A long time. Ten years at
           least.

KATE: Yes, I know.

JAMES: You know?

KATE: Yes.

JAMES: He told you all about it, did he?

KATE: He told me some.

JAMES: Well, there are two sides to every story.

KATE: Sometimes even more.

JAMES: What?

KATE: *(Louder, as if JAMES is hard of hearing)* Sometimes even
             more than two sides... of the same story...

JAMES: Just so you know.

KATE: *(Loud)* Yes, two sides.

JAMES: Right... He's alright like that?

KATE: He's fine.

JAMES: What?

KATE: *(Loud)* He's fine...

JAMES: Good...

PAUSE. *(They are still, looking down at DJ. DJ begins to snore)*

(DJ snores for a few seconds)

BLACKOUT

ACT II, SCENE II

CAT is sitting on a bench on the pedestrian promenade running along the Puxi side of the Huangpu River. She is at a spot close to where the Nanjing Road meets the Bund. The Huangpu River is behind her. There is a bust of Chen Yi nearby. He was a poet and a former mayor of Shanghai, martyred during the Cultural Revolution.

CAT is searching through her purse for something. JAMES appears from stage left. He stops and watches CAT for a moment. JAMES approaches.

JAMES: Lose something?

CAT: No.

JAMES: Need some help?

      (CAT quickly re-orders her purse and closes it. She stands up)

CAT: No.

      (JAMES takes out his handkerchief and dusts off the bench. He signals for CAT to sit down)

JAMES: Sit... Please. *(CAT sits. JAMES sits)* Was I early? Always better to be early than late... As a rule.

      (SHORT PAUSE)

JAMES: I thought it might be a good idea for us to talk... To clear the air... I may be wrong but it seems to me that you're quite serious about DJ... Romantically... If you know what I mean?

PAUSE.

He's a complicated man.

CAT: Yes.

PAUSE.

JAMES: Were you born here? In Shanghai?...

CAT: No...

JAMES: My wife was... Sometimes when I say my wife was born in Shanghai people assume she was Chinese. I can see them hesitate and *wonder* about it... She wasn't... She came back once, in the early '80s. Of course it was a lot different then. Nothing like it is today... They shape you, don't they, the times you grow up in? They did me... I didn't used to think much about it... Now, it's all I think about... At a certain point you start to look back over your life on what happened and wonder why it turned out like it did... Coming back to you, to you and your life... I imagine it couldn't have been easy, being a child, the Cultural Revolution and all... I've read about it... I read a couple of books...

CAT: It was a very hard time.

JAMES: Of course it was... For me, for my generation it was the War. World War II? I was a pilot. I dropped bombs on Germany... I've been to all the reunions. All the big *events*... It's amazing but the emotion is right up there on the surface... I can start to cry just like that... I don't really know why it makes me cry. I didn't lose any *close* friends. We all came through it okay—my whole crew—32 missions... Still, the music, the ceremonies... Vera Lynn... I cry like a baby... So it's a big thing in my life. It always has been... What about you and your *Revolution*... You suffered... The emotion must be there. Yes? It doesn't just evaporate... The emotion...

CAT: We look to the future, that's what we do. We look to the future...

JAMES: I don't know... In my life there's the War... And there's my father.... Like all men, a father's a problem. I don't really like talking about him. I don't like discussing him... He wasn't *nice*... He wasn't a *nice* man really. No one liked him. That's the truth of it... The only thing I know is that when he died, when I went to see his body in the hospital... I *asked* to... I looked down at him, at his face, his mouth, and I wanted to hit him... I never felt that when he was alive... I was really angry. I don't know why. But, clearly, there were some *issues* there... My mother... Well, she could have done better... She was a *debutante*... Her father was *somebody*. No, really, he was in parliament. And he was rich. *Self-made*... A lumberman... She could have done better... Her sisters did... Elsie married an *orthodontist*, for Christ's sake... A couple of them did better... And Euart got the business. That was the son's name: Euart. *(He points down the promenade, stage right)* Is that Mao?... Looks like Mao.

CAT: No, Chen Yi. He was a poet. And the mayor of Shanghai.

JAMES: They all look alike, don't they?... *(He quickly catches himself:)* Revolutionaries... Something about the face...

                SHORT PAUSE. (RONGJI approaches from stage right. He is middle-aged. An old 45. His face is tanned and deeply lined. He wears a grey Mao jacket and cap. His clothes are worn and dirty. He carries his belongings in a few plastic bags. CAT is tense)

JAMES: *(Referring to the approaching RONGJI)*
                Wups... Wups... Easy...

RONGJI: 我要见我的儿子.
            (I want to see my son.)

CAT: 滚开. 不然我就叫警察.
            (Go away or I will call the police.)

RONGJI: *(He takes a photograph out of his pocket and shows CAT)*
            这是我的儿子? 还记得吗, 和他爸爸,妈妈在一
            起. 记得吗?
            (This is my son. Remember? With his mummy and his
            daddy... A long time ago... Remember?)

CAT: 我这就叫警察.
            (I will call the police.)

RONGJI: 求您让我见见他.
            (Please let me see him.)

CAT: 滚开!
            (Go away. Now.)

            *(RONGJI reaches out to touch CAT. CAT slaps his hand
            away)*

            Go away!

            *(RONGJI takes out a piece of rag, blows his nose loudly. The
            photo he showed CAT falls to the ground. CAT does not look
            at him. RONGJI turns and walks off slowly stage right)*

JAMES: Look, he's dropped something. *(JAMES stands and retrieves the photo. He looks at it and then offers it to CAT)* Yours?

CAT: *(She won't look at it)* No, not mine.

JAMES: *(He looks at the photo, smiles, then puts it in his wallet)* Mine, then...

PAUSE.

I don't *like* my son... I can't help it. I've never *liked* him... I just don't feel comfortable with him. I have no problem with his brother or his sister... He's different. Always has been... Do you think that makes me a bad father? Not *liking* my son?... It's the way he looks at me. When I'm talking to him he looks at me and I know he's *thinking*... I know he doesn't *think* much of me... And that's a hard thing to take... His mother loved him. I used to think they were too close. I didn't think it was healthy... She didn't have to take sides. She could have stood back and said it's for you two to work out. I love you both, *equally*. But she didn't. She stood by me... The *family* was never the same. He turned his back on us. Completely... I guess you know all this, don't you? I guess he's told you?

CAT: No.

JAMES: He hasn't told you?

CAT: No.

PAUSE

JAMES: God, I could use a drink... I hate travelling, you know?
            I hate it. Hotel rooms are all the same. I wake up I
            never know where I am. I can't wait to get back to my
            own bed... Course once I'm home I don't know what
            I'll do. I always feel a bit lost. It's a big home—too big
            for one...

PAUSE

Why don't you smile? Smile for me... *(CAT looks at
him)* You don't *smile*. You don't show your teeth... Smile
for me... Please... *(CAT smiles, showing her teeth. He looks
at her teeth. She stops smiling and bows her head)* Oh, I'm
sorry... You shouldn't be embarrassed. There's nothing wrong with your teeth... Nothing a good dentist
couldn't fix... I wasn't born with these you know.
(JAMES shows his teeth) They're not all *mine*... *(If he can
he takes out his teeth to show her)* See? *(JAMES shows her
his teeth; CAT looks at his teeth)* Tell you what. Let me
spoil you... It'll be my little gift to you. No one needs
to know. Okay? Okay?... Will you *let* me do that for
you? *(CAT looks at him and smiles a closed-mouth smile)* ...
A smile is a *powerful* thing...

PAUSE. (JAMES puts his arm around CAT's shoulders. JAMES pulls CAT close to him) SHORT PAUSE.

Kiss me... Go on... Kiss me... On the cheek... Here. *(He offers his cheek. He shuts his eyes and waits)* I'm *waiting...*

PAUSE. (CAT kisses JAMES on the cheek)

JAMES: There now. That wasn't so bad, was it? *Was* it?

CAT: No.

SHORT PAUSE

JAMES: So... Tell me... Who was he? The man in the Mao jacket. A *friend?*...An old friend?...Tell me...

SHORT PAUSE

What's your game, tiger?...

BLACKOUT

ACT II, SCENE III

Same setting as ACT II, SCENE I. DJ is polishing the silver cigarette box. HONGYONG enters and sits at the table and watches DJ. HONGYONG has a cast on his arm. For the first time he appears without sunglasses.

HONGYONG: What are you doing?

DJ: I'm cleaning it.

HONGYONG: Why?

DJ: Because it's dirty.

HONGYONG: Why?

DJ: Because it's old.

HONGYONG: Can I have it?

DJ: No.

HONGYONG: Why?

DJ: Because it's mine...

          PAUSE

          Why don't you do something?

HONGYONG: What?

DJ: Play.

HONGYONG: I don't want to.

DJ: Then learn... Why don't you do more words? Your
              mother made more words for you. See if you can put
              them where they belong.

              *(HONGYONG takes a card from a small pile of labelled
              index cards on the table. Each card has one word on it in black
              ink: LAMP, TABLE, LEG, TELEPHONE etc. HONG-
              YONG takes the first card and tapes it to the telephone)*

HONGYONG: 对吗?
              (Correct?)

DJ: *(He looks up)* That's right... Keep going...

              *(CAT enters the flat. She carries a plastic bag and a handful
              of mail. She puts the mail down on the table in front of DJ.
              DJ continues cleaning the cigarette box. HONGYONG con-
              tinues to tape index cards to objects. Each time he tapes a card
              to something he looks to DJ for confirmation)*

DJ: *(Referring to the mail)* Anything interesting?

CAT: What?

DJ: In the mail?

CAT: I didn't look.

DJ: Why not?

CAT: It's your mail.

               *(PAUSE. HONGYONG waits for DJ to confirm a card he
               has taped to the table leg. The card reads: LEG)*

HONGYONG: 喂!
               (Hey!)

DJ: *(He looks at card)* Yes. You're right. But can you find
               another example?

HONGYONG: Another example?

DJ: Sometimes words have several meanings. Tables have
               legs. What else has legs?

HONGYONG: Tell me.

DJ: You won't learn if I tell you. *(To CAT)* And don't you
               tell him. Let him figure it out.

(DJ begins to open the mail. CAT catches HONGYONG's attention and indicates her leg. She then puts her finger to her lips. HONGYONG giggles)

What's so funny?

CAT: Nothing. *(HONGYONG giggles)*

DJ: What are you two up to?

HONGYONG: I know it.

DJ: Know what?

HONGYONG: *(He takes the label off the leg of the table)* This is a leg... *(He tapes the label to his leg)* And this is a leg.

DJ: Smarty pants.

HONGYONG: What is smarty pants?

DJ: You. You're a smarty pants.

HONGYONG: No, I'm not.

DJ: Keep going. Get another one.

HONGYONG: *(He takes an index card, looks at it, frowns and says)* What is this?

(He holds up the card. It says: LUCKY)

DJ: That's a hard one. It's not an object. You can't tape it to something.

HONGYONG: What does it mean?

DJ: It means good fortune... It means someone who has good fortune.

(HONGYONG tapes the index card to DJ's back)

You think I'm lucky?

HONGYONG: Yes.

DJ: Why?

HONGYONG: You have a father.

(DJ pulls the index card off his back and places it on the table)

My father is dead. He died before I was born. I don't remember him.

DJ: No memories are better than bad memories.

HONGYONG: I would like some memories.

(DJ opens an envelope. The envelope is empty except for a small photograph. He stares at the photo. It is the photo JAMES put in his wallet in ACT II, SCENE II. HONGYONG takes another index card. He tapes it to DJ's back. The card reads FAMILY)

DJ: *(Reacting to the card HONGYONG is taping to his back)*
What are you doing?

HONGYONG: It's not lucky. It's a different word.

(HONGYONG giggles. DJ holds the photo up for CAT to see)

DJ: What's this?

CAT: What?

DJ: A photograph.

(HONGYONG giggles loudly)

HONGYONG: Guess... Guess the word.

DJ: Shall I show him?

HONGYONG: Show me what?

CAT: 到你房间去!
                (Go to your room!)

HONGYONG: Can I see it?

DJ: You said he was dead. You said he died before
                Hongyong was born.

HONGYONG: Who?

DJ: You lied.

CAT: I didn't think I had a choice.

DJ: When were you going to tell us?

HONGYONG: Let me see.

DJ: No.

HONGYONG: Please, can I see? Please?

CAT: I thought it was better if he thought he was dead.

HONGYONG: Who?

DJ: You lied to both of us.

BRIEF PAUSE. (HONGYONG stands still, waiting)

DJ: *(To HONGYONG)* What do you want? What do you want from me?... *(DJ reaches around and pulls off the card FAMILY. He stares at the card for a few seconds then crumples the card and throws it on the ground)*

DJ: I'm not your father... Understand?... Understand?!

HONGYONG: *(He runs into his bedroom stage left slamming the door behind him)*

PAUSE

BLACKOUT

ACT II, SCENE IV

JAMES' hotel room. A few days have passed. JAMES wears socks on his feet and a robe over an undershirt and boxers. He sits in an armchair. He has been reading the International Herald Tribune. *Pieces of the newspaper are scattered on the floor around his chair. CAT stands at the end of his bed. His bed is unmade.*

JAMES: Please, make yourself comfortable.

                PAUSE

CAT: He told me to leave.

JAMES: He's thrown you out?

CAT: Yes.

JAMES: So, what will you do? Where will you go?

CAT: I don't know.

JAMES: You'll go home...

CAT: I can't go home.

JAMES: Why not?

CAT: I *left*.

SHORT PAUSE

JAMES: What do you want from me?

CAT: You could talk to him.

JAMES: What happened?

CAT: He says I lied.

JAMES: Did you?

CAT: Yes.

JAMES: What can I do?

CAT: You're his father.

JAMES: That's never worked.

PAUSE

Tell me. The man by the river. The man in the photo.
That's your husband?

CAT: We're divorced.

JAMES: What does he want from you?

CAT: He wants to see Hongyong.

JAMES: It's his son. Of course he wants to see his son.

CAT: Hongyong isn't his son.

JAMES: I don't understand.

CAT: I fell in love with a man in my village. He was married
                and had a child. He said he was unhappy and wanted to
                leave his wife. I became pregnant. He refused to leave
                his wife. My parents were very ashamed. They
                arranged for me to marry Rongji. The man in the
                photo. They said if I didn't marry him they would take
                Hongyong away. So I married him. When Hongyong
                was two I asked for a divorce. When I got the divorce
                I ran away.

JAMES: Hell's bells, that's a story!

CAT: Yes.

JAMES: Is it true?

CAT: Yes.

JAMES: So he's found you.

CAT: Yes.

JAMES: You told this to DJ?

CAT: No.

JAMES: Why not?

CAT: What good would it do?

JAMES: He might understand.

CAT: Understand what?

JAMES: Why you lied... Sometimes if you understand the reasons behind a lie you can forgive the lie itself... In fact, knowing why someone lies makes it no longer a lie, it makes it something else.

CAT: What?

JAMES: A *version* of the truth...

            PAUSE. (JAMES stands and moves toward CAT)

            He's complicated.

CAT: Yes.

JAMES: He's sensitive.

CAT: Yes.

JAMES: He had an *audition*...

            PAUSE. (JAMES moves closer to CAT)

            Look at you... You *deserve* to be loved...

CAT: Would you take care of me?

JAMES: I could.

CAT: Give me a home?

JAMES: I can provide. I know how to do that.

CAT: I could be your happiness...

JAMES: What kind of woman are you? I'm baffled... For me,
            I'm baffled...

CAT: I'm a woman who wants a better life.

JAMES: You want a dream?

CAT: Yes.

JAMES: Dreams are good... Even old men have dreams...

PAUSE. (There is a knock on the door. They look at the door and then at each other) SHORT PAUSE. (There is another louder knock on the door).

Perhaps you should skedaddle.

CAT: What?

JAMES: Hide... They probably just want to make up the room. Wait in there *(motioning toward the door to the washroom)* until I get rid of them.

(There is another knock on the door)

Coming! Coming. *(To CAT)* Hide. I'll let you know when the coast is clear.

CAT: The coast?

JAMES: When it's *safe*.

(CAT gathers her things and hides in the washroom. He opens the door a crack)

Yes?... Oh... Do come in. *(JAMES opens the door; KATE breezes in)* Yes, sorry. I was just resting.

KATE: *(Her hair is done and she wears makeup. She's dressed to impress)* So sorry to barge in on you like this... So

117

sorry... I was in the neighborhood. I thought if you were free...

JAMES: How kind. Do come in.

KATE: I'm not disturbing you, am I?

JAMES: No, I—

KATE: I have a proposition for you. An idea. A business opportunity.

JAMES: Oh?

KATE: Look at me... I'm an old lady. No one bothers an old lady...

JAMES: I'm confused.

KATE: I don't get searched. They let me through. I smuggle 'objets'... It's how I survive... Just... And I thought you might like to participate?

JAMES: Hell's bells...

KATE: You don't have to decide right now. You'll want to think about it. Mull it over.

JAMES: Oh? Really?

KATE: Of course. I'd expect nothing less... You're the entre-
           preneur...

JAMES: Yes... I am...

KATE: I thought we could go to the Peace Hotel.

JAMES: The *Peace* Hotel?

KATE: I thought we could have tea. Or something stronger...
           To discuss the opportunity... If you're not busy?

JAMES: No. I'm not. Actually I—

KATE: You're free then?

JAMES: Yes.

KATE: Don't say yes if you don't want to.

JAMES: I wouldn't.

           PAUSE

KATE: I'm blushing.

JAMES: Yes, you are.

KATE: I'm sorry. Excuse me...

JAMES: No excuse necessary...

                (The door to the bathroom opens. CAT enters the room, clos-
                ing the bathroom door behind her)

KATE: What are you doing here?

CAT: I'm going to Canada.

KATE: Going to Canada? What are you talking about? *(To*
                James) What is she talking about?

                (CAT kisses JAMES on the cheek. She walks to the door of
                the room, stops and looks back at KATE)

CAT: He's taking me to Canada.

KATE: *(Stunned)* Canada?...

CAT: *(To JAMES)* Aren't you?

                PAUSE

JAMES: *(To KATE)* Well... I know an *orthodontist*... *(To CAT)*
                Show her...

                (CAT smiles broadly at KATE, showing her teeth)

KATE: I see... *(quietly)* Dear God... I feel such a fool...

PAUSE

BLACKOUT

ACT II, SCENE V

A few days later. DJ'S flat. DJ, KATE and SAM are drinking tea. There are two suitcases sitting by the door.

DJ: *(He takes the photo of his mother's house from his wallet and shows it to SAM)* That was taken in 1929... Of course, it's changed...

KATE: I'll say!...

DJ: I wanted to get inside. So I started taking pictures of the outside. First, from across the street. Then closer. The camera was flashing. It brought them out. Finally, a little girl, maybe 12 or 13 appeared. She came up to me and in perfect English asked me what I was doing. I told her that this was my mother's house. She told her parents and the other residents. There must be 20 people living there, a half-dozen families. So they gave me a tour... The place is falling to pieces. It hasn't been painted in decades. Filthy... All the public areas are a mess. The halls, the doors to the street—anything that's shared is ignored. But if you get inside someone's space, the flat they've carved out for themselves, it's impeccable. Privately, they're as proud about their living space as anyone, anywhere... But no one cares about the public spaces, the shared space. What does that mean?... What's that about?

SAM: Are you asking me?

DJ: Yes. I'm asking you.

SAM: The public space is not their responsibility.

DJ: Then whose responsibility is it?

SAM: Well, it's the government's responsibility.

SHORT PAUSE

DJ: They all thought I had some authority. They pointed
                      out the leaking roof, the rotting stairs and the peeling
                      paint and asked when I would be making repairs.
                      They've been waiting for someone to take responsibil-
                      ity since 1949... That's my impression.

SAM: No, someone's responsible. I'll look into it. I'll find
                      out.

SHORT PAUSE

                      Are they married yet?

DJ: Yes. They've done the civil thing so she can get her
                      papers. When they get back to Canada they'll do
                      something grand.

SAM: I don't understand.

DJ: What don't you understand?

SAM: You shared the same bed.

DJ: Yes.

SAM: Now she shares your father's bed.

DJ: Yes... Probably...

SAM: Sometimes I think I understand people from the West
            and then you do something that makes me feel I know
            nothing.

            SHORT PAUSE

KATE: Canada's a better place for the boy.

SAM: Why?

KATE: The politics, the schools, the health care, for heaven's
            sake!

SAM: But his family and his history are here.

KATE: You'd deny him a better life?

SAM: Why would it be a better life? He can grow fat and stu-
                pid here as easily as he could in Canada...

KATE: Of course, you believe in the *destiny* of China.

SAM: Yes. I do. One day China will be united and strong. A
                great nation under one flag.

KATE: And Tiananmen?

SAM: If you believe in China then you see Tiananmen as an
                accident... If you do not believe in China then you
                believe there is worse to come... the Handover will fail
                and 1997 will be the beginning of the end... You think
                he will have a better life in Canada? What better life
                could he ask for than to play a role in the future of
                China?

                (The doorbell buzzes)

DJ: It's my father. He's come to collect her things.

KATE: What about Hongyong?

DJ: He's staying with me until they fly to Canada.

                (The doorbell buzzes again)

                Come in!

(JAMES enters)

JAMES: Hello... Hello...

KATE: Congratulations.

JAMES: Oh... Thank you... Very kind...

KATE: I'm sorry I missed the ceremony.

JAMES: Are you feeling better?

KATE: Much better, thank you.

JAMES: It was very simple. Nothing grand. Lovely.

KATE: I'm very happy for you.

JAMES: Thank you.

DJ: Her bags are there.

JAMES: Oh... Good... I...

SHORT PAUSE

DJ: What?

JAMES: Well, I...

PAUSE

KATE: *(To DJ)* Should we leave?... Do you want us to leave? Perhaps we should go?

DJ: No. Stay... He's not staying long... He's come for her bags. Haven't you?

JAMES: Yes... Listen... I wanted to say... Well, we weren't a good match, as father and son, were we?... I wasn't a *good* father. I accept that. I made mistakes. I'm sorry. But I did my best. I really did. I wasn't perfect. I had problems. And you paid for those problems... I'm a different man now. I've changed. I know what's important. I think I can be a good husband now. And a good father... If it comes to that.

DJ: What do you mean, "if it comes to that"?

JAMES: Oh, well, there are complications. With the boy. With taking him to Canada.

KATE: *Complications?*

JAMES: His father doesn't want him to go. Can't blame him really. How's he going to visit? How's he going to play a role in the boy's life from 5,000 miles away? No, it's better he stays here. Better all round.

KATE: She's going to let him go back to that village?

JAMES: We'll keep in touch. We'll visit. We'll send *gifts*...

KATE: Shit.

JAMES: *(Pointing at the suitcases by the door)* This is everything?

DJ: You can't do that...

JAMES: His father will be by to get him about 11 tomorrow morning. Is that convenient?...

DJ: You can't do it.

JAMES: What are you talking about?

DJ: You can't play with his life like that.

JAMES: I'm not *playing* with his life. It's just how it's worked out, that's all. No fault, no foul.

DJ: It's not fair.

JAMES: Will you have him *ready*?... *Please*...

DJ: You can't just send him back to the country.

JAMES: What do you *propose?*

DJ: He can stay here. He can live here and go to school. I'll
           take care of him.

JAMES: You're not thinking right... This is *China*. It's not your
           fucking country.

DJ: I'll adopt him. I could adopt him. *(To KATE)* I could
           do that, couldn't I?

KATE: I don't know...

JAMES: What, are you crazy? You're *queer*. They won't let you
           near him...

           PAUSE

KATE: He's not an orphan. He has a father. I'm sorry, dear. I
           don't think you could adopt him.

           SHORT PAUSE

JAMES: You think I don't know?...I've always known...

           PAUSE

(JAMES stands beside the suitcases. He picks up the bags. To KATE) It's been a pleasure...

KATE: Goodbye.

JAMES: *(To SAM)* Nice meeting you.

SAM: Goodbye.

             PAUSE

JAMES: *(He turns to exit but the door is closed. He turns back)* Could someone open the door?... *Please?*

             SHORT PAUSE

DJ: Do you need some help with those?

JAMES: Just the door... Please... *(DJ opens the door for JAMES. JAMES moves to exit but stops. To DJ)* Good luck...

             SHORT PAUSE

DJ: You never said anything.

JAMES: Would it have made a difference?

             PAUSE

DJ: It might have...

             (JAMES exits. DJ shuts the door behind him).

             SILENCE

             BLACKOUT

ACT II, SCENE VI

DJ's flat. The next day. KATE sits at the table. HONGYONG is removing the index cards labelling objects in the flat. He removes a card and hands it to KATE. Every time he gives KATE a card she calls out the word and then places the card on a pile of cards on the table.

	(HONGYONG takes a card off a chair and brings it to KATE).
KATE:	*(She takes the card from HONGYONG)* Chair. *(HONGYONG removes the card from the window and brings it to KATE)* Window... *(He takes the card off the door and brings it to KATE)* Door...
	(DJ enters. He carries the silver cigarette box. He watches KATE and HONGYONG)
DJ:	What are you doing?
KATE:	He's returning your language.
	PAUSE
DJ:	All packed?
	(HONGYONG does not acknowledge DJ. He takes the label off the clock and hands it to KATE)

KATE: Clock...

               PAUSE. (DJ offers HONGYONG the silver cigarette box)

DJ: I want to give you this. As a gift.

HONGYONG: It's yours.

DJ: Yes. But now I want to give it to you.

               *PAUSE. (DJ offers it to HONGYONG. HONGYONG
               takes it. Holds it)*

KATE: What do you say?

HONGYONG: Thank you.

KATE: Why don't you put it in your suitcase?

               (HONGYONG exits) PAUSE

               That was kind...

DJ: I want him to remember me.

KATE: Why wouldn't he?

               SHORT PAUSE

DJ: How are we going to do this?

KATE: What do you mean?

DJ: How do we do it?

(HONGYONG enters. He carries a suitcase. CANADA is written in white block letters across the side of the suitcase: a child's hand writing. He places it by the door) PAUSE

HONGYONG: What's wrong?

DJ: Nothing's wrong.

KATE: Come. Sit down.

HONGYONG: Why?

DJ: Please sit down.

KATE: On the chair. Here. Sit here.

HONGYONG: Have I been a bad boy?

KATE: No. You're a wonderful boy.

SHORT PAUSE

DJ: I have to tell you something.

HONGYONG: What?

DJ: Your father will be here soon.

HONGYONG: My father?

DJ: Yes.

HONGYONG: My father is dead.

DJ: He's not dead. He's coming here. He'll be here soon.

KATE: He's been looking for you for a long time.

HONGYONG: How do you know?

DJ: He's travelled all over China looking for you.

KATE: He's come to take you home.

HONGYONG: But I'm going to Canada.

DJ: He'll be here soon. Any minute.

HONGYONG: He can come and visit me in Canada if he wants. It's a
            big house. He can have his own room.

KATE: You're not going to Canada.

HONGYONG: Yes I am. My suitcase is packed. Look. It says Canada.

(HONGYONG goes into his room shutting the door behind him)

SHORT PAUSE. (The doorbell buzzes)

DJ: Come in... *(He waits and then moves to answer the door. He opens the door. RONGJI enters. This is the same middle-aged man from ACT II, SCENE II. RONGJI wears a worn grey Mao jacket and cap)*

RONGJI: *(To DJ)* Ni-hao... *(He offers his hand to DJ)*

DJ: Ni-hao ma... *(They shake hands)*

RONGJI: 我来带我儿子回家.

DJ: What's he saying?

KATE: He's come for Hongyong.

DJ: What do I do?

KATE: You better get him.

(DJ knocks on the door to HONGYONG's room. He waits and then knocks again. He calls out his name)

DJ: Hongyong?

                   (RONGJI suddenly pushes past DJ and knocks loudly on
                   HONGYONG's door)

RONGJI: Hongyong! Hongyong!

DJ: Wait. Slow down... Please.

KATE: *(Translates for RONGJI)*
                   等等. 请你慢点.
                   (He nods and steps back from the bedroom door)

RONGJI: *(He takes a small photo out of his pocket. He shows it to DJ*
                   and KATE. He explains in Chinese; KATE translates).
                   这是我儿子

KATE: (This is my son. My beautiful boy. Every day I prayed
                   to God that my Hongyong would come back to me.)

RONGJI: *(He holds up the photo)*
                   这是我儿子
                   (This is *my* son.)

DJ: Yes. I understand. *(To KATE)* Tell him I understand.

                   (KATE translates)
                   他懂.
                   (RONGJI understands)

RONGJI: *(In English)* Rule of Law... Rule of Law... Yes?

DJ: Yes... Rule of Law.

RONGJI: 我是个农民. 我没文化.我以前很快活!

KATE: *(KATE translates)* I am a farmer. I am not educated...

RONGJI: 我有过老婆,有过儿子. 一个心疼的儿子.

KATE: I was happy. I had a wife and a son. A beautiful boy. His
            smile filled me with happiness...

RONGJI: 他一笑我就高兴.有一天我下地回来, 他们不见了.
            家里空空的, 她娘俩儿都不见了.

KATE: One day I came home from work and they were gone.
            My house was empty. My wife and my son were gone.

RONGJI: 过去8年我天天都在找儿子.

KATE: I have never stopped looking for my son.

RONGJI: 8年了, 我天天向神祈祷, 求他帮我儿子带回家.

KATE: For eight years, every day, I have prayed to God that
            my son will come home...

RONGJI: *(In English)* I am a Christian. I pray to God. Yes?
               (Continuing in Chinese) 这下可算找到了！谢谢您！

KATE: *(Translating)* And now I have found him... Thank you.

RONGJI: *(In English)* Thank you.

               *(HONGYONG enters. He carries another suitcase. CANA-
               DA is written on the side of the suitcase in white block letters.
               He takes the suitcase to the front door)*

KATE: Hongyong, this is your father.

HONGYONG: He's a peasant. *My* father is not a peasant.

RONGJI: *(He takes a small toy truck out of his pocket and holds it up to
               HONGYONG. In English)* Daddy bring you present.

DJ: He's your father. And he wants to take you home.

HONGYONG: I think I will go to Canada... Tell him. Please tell him.

RONGJI: *(Referring to suitcases by the door. In English)* Yes?...Yes?

DJ: Yes, those are his.

RONGJI: *(He speaks in Chinese to HONGYONG)*
               Hongyong? Hongyong? 这么大了？

DJ: What's he saying?

KATE: He said, "Hongyong. Such a big boy."

RONGJI: 我可想死你了.

KATE: I have missed you so much.

RONGJI: 我从来都没放放弃希望.

KATE: I have never given up hope.

RONGJI: 我每天都向神祈祷, 祈祷宏勇能回到我身边

KATE: Every day I prayed to God that my Hongyong would
               come back to me.

RONGJI: 瞧,

KATE: Look.

RONGJI: *(He takes a small photo of HONGYONG out of his wallet)*
               这是你, 我的宝贝儿子. 你还记得吗?

KATE: This is you. My little boy... Do you remember?

RONGJI: *(He holds the photo in his two hands and kisses it)*
               我每天都为我儿子祈祷

KATE: Every day I prayed to find my son.

RONGJI: *(In English)* My son... My son...

DJ: Yes. Your son.

               SHORT PAUSE

RONGJI: Rule of Law... Yes? Rule of Law...

DJ: It's not what he wants.

KATE: He's Chinese. This is his country. These are his people.

DJ: You think this is right?

KATE: Honestly? I think he should be with his mother. Wherever she is.

DJ: She doesn't love him... She doesn't care.

KATE: No. But this man loves him... You can see that, can't you? He really loves him...

               (HONGYONG re-enters. He carries his coat over his arm)

RONGJI: *(In English)* We go home? Yes?

DJ: *(To HONGYONG)* I'm sorry.

                   *(DJ takes the coat from HONGYONG and holds it open for
                   HONGYONG to slip into. HONGYONG slips his arms
                   into the coat. RONGJI notices the silver cigarette box in the
                   coat pocket. RONGJI lifts out the box)*

RONGJI: *(In English to HONGYONG:)* You steal? *(HONG-
                   YONG looks up at RONGJI without expression. RONGJI
                   strikes HONGYONG hard across the face. HONGYONG
                   falls back onto the floor)* Bad boy! *(RONGJI hands DJ the
                   silver box. He says in English)* Sorry... So sorry. Mistake.
                   *(HONGYONG stands up slowly. His nose is bleeding.
                   RONGJI grabs HONGYONG by the scruff of the neck
                   and yells at him in Chinese:* 你给你爸爸丢脸！当起小偷了？
                   这是你妈的血. 你妈... (You shame your father like
                   this? A thief? This is your mother's blood. Your
                   mother.)

KATE: Stop! Enough! *(In Chinese)* 别再说了 (Please stop!)

DJ: It's a gift. It's his. I want him to have it.

RONGJI: *(DJ offers the box to RONGJI. RONGJI looks at the box
                   and then at HONGYONG. In English)* My son does not
                   need. Okay? Okay?

DJ: *(He offers the box to HONGYONG. HONGYONG takes the box looks at it and then places it on the table)* I want you to have it. A gift... To remember me.

RONGJI: *(RONGJI clips HONGYONG at the back of his head. In English)* Bad boy... You say thank you! You say thank you!

HONGYONG: Thank you.

RONGJI: You say thank you to nice man. Go. Say it.

HONGYONG: Thank you.

DJ: You're welcome.

PAUSE. (KATE offers HONGYONG a white linen hand-kerchief to wipe the blood from his nose. RONGJI raises his hand to block her and shakes his head no. He reaches into his pocket to take out the scrap of rag he used to blow his nose in ACT II, SCENE II. He hands the rag to HONGYONG. HONGYONG looks at the filthy rag and then slowly wipes the blood from his nose)

RONGJI: You say thank you.

HONGYONG: Thank you...

RONGJI: Yes. Thank you. *(He extends his hand to DJ)* Thank you. *(He shakes KATE'S hand and says thank you to her.*

HONGYONG stands still and silent, his head bowed. RONGJI moves toward the front door. He turns and snaps at HONGYONG) Come now. I take you home... Come. *(RONGJI holds the door open. HONGYONG picks up his suitcases and exits without looking at DJ or KATE. RONGJI nods goodbye and closes the door behind him)*

SHORT PAUSE

:   *(DJ holds the cigarette box. He looks at the box. He opens it and closes it. He doesn't know what to do)*

SHORT PAUSE

KATE: *(She picks up the pile of index cards)* The words... He forgot his words...

PAUSE

BLACKOUT

EPILOGUE

Same setting as ACT II, SCENE II. KATE is waiting for someone. She holds a dog leash in her hands. She looks up and down the promenade. She calls out.

KATE: Ruby?... Ruby... Rubaloo?... Damn you!... Where is that dog?

               (SAM enters. He watches KATE as she looks for her dog. He smiles)

SAM: Looking for something?

KATE: What?... No...

SAM: How are you?

KATE: Fine... Fine...

SAM: Your dog?

KATE: Off doing her business...

SAM: Oh.

               SHORT PAUSE

KATE: So...

SAM: Yes?

KATE: What are they *thinking*?

              SHORT PAUSE

SAM: Who?

KATE: Your 'bosses.'

SAM: They never tell me what they're thinking.

KATE: What are they *saying*?

SAM: If I'm lucky they tell me about their children.

KATE: I don't understand.

SAM: If they're angry or unhappy they say nothing. They give
              instruction without comment... If they're pleased with
              me they talk about their children...

KATE: People are funny.

              PAUSE

SAM: They're sending me to London.

KATE: A posting?

SAM: Yes.

KATE   That means something, doesn't it?

SAM: It means they trust me.

KATE: Well done.

SAM: Perhaps.

KATE: They must be happy with your work?

SAM: They're not unhappy...

KATE: Congratulations.

SAM: Thank you.

KATE: A feather in your cap.

SAM: What does that mean?

KATE: A job well done.

SAM: A good thing?

KATE: Yes.

                SHORT PAUSE

KATE: Ruby!

SHORT PAUSE.

SAM: And you? Your 'bosses'? Are they happy with your 'work'?

KATE: I'm still here.

SAM: *Poised...*

KATE: Yes.

PAUSE

Well... *London...* Makes sense... the Handover *looms...*

PAUSE

SAM: By the way, this will be our last meeting. Our last *formal* meeting.

KATE: You're being replaced?

SAM: Yes.

KATE: Permanently?

SAM: Yes. You'll have someone *new*.

KATE: A new contact? A new... relationship?... Oh, I hate
              this...

SAM: A woman.

KATE: A woman?! Christ!

SAM: What's wrong with a woman?

KATE: But they're the worst. She'll have me memorizing pass-
              words and secret handshakes.

SAM: I'm sure you'll get along just fine.

KATE: You've met her?

SAM: No. But I know about her. I've heard about her.

              PAUSE

KATE: Everything's changing.

SAM: All the time.

KATE: Any advice then? On how to handle her?

SAM: Tell the truth.

KATE: The truth! I never tell the truth.

SAM: You don't?

KATE: God, no. I tell them what I think they want to hear—
             no more, no less. I offer a *version* of the truth...

SAM: The industry's changing. Protocols evolving...

KATE: Do you tell them everything?

SAM: Everything. I don't interpret, I just report.

KATE: Must be something *generational*...

SAM: It's too complicated to do anything else. There's too
             much information.

KATE: *(She is becoming anxious)* Ruby?... Ruby... Come here, old
             girl.

             PAUSE

             How's our Canadian friend?

KATE: Which one?

SAM: The writer.

KATE: He's in Tianjin.

SAM: What's he up to?

KATE: Who's asking?

SAM: Me... nothing *official* here.

KATE: He sent me a postcard. A "Hi how are you I'm doing
            fine;" no *news* to speak of. Nothing interesting...
            Nothing to *share*.

SAM: You helped him find his mother's house.

KATE: Probably gone now, probably demolished.

SAM: He wanted to know who was responsible for the pub-
            lic areas... The filthy hallways. The rotting stairs...

KATE: Peeling paint...

SAM: Leaking roof...

KATE: Yes, you were going to find out...

SAM: The government's responsible.

KATE: So, they're remiss?

SAM: Yes. But why is the government remiss?

KATE: Resources stretched thin...

SAM: I think it's more serious than that.

KATE: Oh?

SAM: They see the government as completely separate from themselves. They don't see the government as *of* the people and *for* the people.

KATE: This is a revelation, is it?

SAM: It's not a good thing.

KATE   No, it isn't... They're not connected. There's no *relationship*.

SAM: No, there isn't. There's nothing holding it together. The only relationship possible is a paternalistic one. If that breaks down, if there's a loss of faith...

KATE   Chaos.

SAM: Yes...

              PAUSE

KATE: Where in God's name is my dog? My Ruby!

          PAUSE

KATE: A woman?

SAM: Yes.

KATE: London?

SAM: Yes.

KATE: When?

SAM: Soon...

KATE: You'll love it... just love it.

SAM: I know...

KATE: You might want to stay.

SAM: In London?

KATE: You might never come back.

SAM: I'll come back.

KATE: You never know.

SAM: I know.

KATE: Do you?

SAM: I believe in China. Remember?

KATE: The Handover *looms*...

SAM: I *believe* in China.

KATE: Ruby!

SAM: I think she's lost.

KATE: No. She's here... She must be...

SAM: Do you have a licence?

KATE: For the dog?

SAM: Yes.

KATE: No.

SAM: Why not?

KATE: Can you help me?

SAM: You should have a licence.

KATE: Please?...

SAM: You should have a licence...It's the law...

KATE: But she's missing.

           PAUSE

SAM: Good luck...

KATE: Please?...

           (SAM exits. Kate cries out)

           Ruby!

           PAUSE

           BLACKOUT

THE END

THE AUTHOR WOULD LIKE TO ACKNOWLEDGE THE SUPPORT OF THE

Factory Theatre
Ontario Arts Council
Tarragon Theatre

AND FOR THE GENEROUS TIME, ADVICE AND INPUT OF

Lothaire Bluteau
Barry Callaghan
Dr. Virginia Griffin & John Craig
Mike DeNoma
David Ferry
John Flarity
Branko Gorjup
Sheila Hill
Karen Hosein
Tess Johnston
MT Kelly
Diana Kuprel
Bill Lane
Jeremy Ransom
Fiona Reid
Richard Rose
Ruth Vandenberg
Seán Virgo
Lilly Wong
Haiyan Zhang

Lawrence Jeffery, of Niagara-on-the-Lake in Ontario, has had his dramas performed, published, and translated since 1982. He is also a co-founder and a director of the Impossible Odds Foundation, which raises money to support children in need internationally. Exile Editions brought out his *Four Plays* and *Who Look in Stove*.

For more, see: www.flyingarmchair.com

Photograph by Gabriela Campos